rea

GUIDE TO

BANK ACCOUNTS & CREDIT CARDS

ILYCE R. GLINK

Real U Guides

Publisher and CEO:
Steve Schultz

Editor-in-Chief:
Megan Stine

Art Director:
C.C. Krohne

Designer:
David Jackson

Illustration:
Mike Strong

Production Manager:
Alice Todd

Associate Editor:
Liesa Abrams

Editorial Assistant:
Cody O. Stine

Copy Editor:
Leslie Fears

Library of Congress Control Number: 2004090906

ISBN: 0-9744159-4-4

First Edition
10 9 8 7 6 5 4 3 2 1

Published by
Real U, Inc.
2582 Centerville Rosebud Rd.
Loganville, GA 30052

www.realuguides.com

Real U is a trademark of Real U, Inc.

Photo Credits:
Cover and Page 1: Digital Vision/Getty Images; Page 3: Jason Dewey/Getty Images; Page 4: Writing a check, Ryan McVay/Getty Images; Girl at ATM, Thinkstock/Getty Images; Page 5: Shredder, ArtToday; Young man, Alexander Walter/Getty Images; Woman jumps for joy, Plush Studios/Getty Images; Checkbook, PhotoLink/Getty Images; Page 6: Victoria Yee/Getty Images; Page 7: Chabruken/Getty Images; Page 8: Tickets, Megan Stine; Concert, ArtToday; Page 10: Alexander Walter/Getty Images; Page 12: Jason Dewey/Getty Images; Page 13: ArtToday; Page 14: Jason Dewey/Getty Images; Page 15: ArtToday; Page 16: Thinkstock/Getty Images; Page 17: RubberBall Productions/Getty Images; Page 18: Ryan McVay/Getty Images; Page 19: Ryan McVay/Getty Images; Page 20: PhotoLink/Getty Images; Page 21: Ryan McVay/Getty Images; Page 23: Blank check, C Squared Studioss/Getty Images; Checkbook register, Steve Schultz; Page 25: Megan Stine; Page 26: Nancy R. Cohen/Getty Images; Page 28: SW Productions/Getty Images; Page 29: Alexander Walter/Getty Images; Page 30: Photodisc Collection/Getty Images; Page 31: ArtToday; Page 32: Janis Christie/Getty Images; Page 34: Digital Vision/Getty Images; Page 35: Ryan McVay/Getty Images; Page 36: Digital Vision/Getty Images; Page 38-39: Legal pad background, Photodisc Collection/Getty Images; Page 38: Woman at ATM, ArtToday; Page 40: Rob Melnychuk/Getty Images; Page 43: Digital Vision/Getty Images; Page 44: Woman looking at bill, ArtToday; Television, Ryan McVay/Getty Images; Page 45: ArtToday; Page 46: ArtToday; Page 47: Digital Vision/Getty Images; Page 48: Ryan McVay/Getty Images; Page 50: Plush Studios/Getty Images; Page 51: Mike Powell/Getty Images; Page 53: Tow-away sign, ArtToday; Page 54: Donna Day/Getty Images; Page 56: Don Farrall/Getty Images; Page 59: ArtToday; Page 60: Digital Vision/Getty Images; Page 61: Digital Vision/Getty Images; Page 62: Digital Vision/Getty Images; Page 63: Mike Powell/Getty Images.

realU

GUIDE TO

BANK ACCOUNTS & CREDIT CARDS

ILYCE R. GLINK

You've got the paycheck, and all you can think is . . . now what?

Spend it? Yeah. Save some? You wish. Get more? Definitely…but how? Sometimes it seems like the toughest thing about money is getting some in the first place. But the truth is, that's only step one. Because once you've got a little cash, it's all about holding on to it, and even—if you're lucky—watching it multiply right before your eyes.

You don't have to be a financial wizard (or any other kind) to take control of your personal finances. But you do need to know some basic facts about how to get the most bang for your buck. How do you know which bank is right for you? Do you need debit cards, credit cards, or both? And how do you get a credit card if you've never had credit before?

If you're short on answers, there's no need to panic. Just check out this guide for everything you need to know to keep yourself in the black.

And welcome to realU

GUIDE TO BANK ACCOUNTS & CREDIT CARDS
TABLE OF CONTENTS

QUIZ: Can You Be Trusted With a Checkbook?.....................6

All About Checking and Savings Accounts......................11
    How to Choose and Open a Bank Account
    ATM Safety
    Banking and Paying Bills Online
    Paperwork: What to Shred and What to Keep

Plastic! All About Credit Cards...........................33
    How to Get Your First Card
    Credit Card Dictionary
    Debit vs. Credit Cards
    Not My Coffee Table: How to Dispute a Charge

How to Manage Credit So You Really Score 49

Managing Debt:
How to Pay It Off as Quickly as Possible 57

Your Money and Your Life: What to Do When.................61

QUIZ:

So you walk into a bank to open a checking account, and an hour later you walk out with a tote bag, a phone shaped like a football, a lime green checkbook cover, and checks emblazoned with your name and address over backgrounds of mountain views, the ocean, Scooby Doo, and kittens—you got the "variety" pack.

eating out—again!

And all that's nothing compared to the leopard print credit card you've got coming in the mail any day now. Who knew banking was so easy—and so brightly colored? Hold it—we're happy for you about your free gifts, but do you really know what you just signed up for? Before you sign on any dotted lines, take this quiz and find out if you're ready for financial independence.

TRUSTED WITH A CHECKBOOK?

1.

It's your favorite day of the week—payday. In a flash you deposit your check, withdraw some spending cash, and get set for big weekend plans. Over the 3-day weekend, you either write checks or use your debit card for a dinner with friends, your rent, the cover at a club, breakfast and coffee, movie tickets, Sunday brunch, and an adorable leopard print handbag which you couldn't resist—it matches your new credit card! When the week-end is over, one look inside the checkbook register reveals:

A. The phone number of the guy you met in line at the ATM.

B. Careful records of every check you paid—including the check numbers–along with every withdrawal and debit card purchase, so you're up to date on what your true balance is, not just how much money the bank thinks you have.

C. Hmm…checkbook register… checkbook register…where is that checkbook register thingie?

2.

You come home one day to find a letter waiting that says you've been approved for a credit card with no interest and no annual fee. Nice. You:

A. Sign on the dotted line and mail back the application ASAP, before the company changes its mind.

B. Read the letter carefully and notice that the zero interest is just an "introductory rate" that jumps to 19% after two months. Shred the letter before you toss it.

C. Check your horoscope and decide you must have been chosen for this lucky gift because the stars are aligned. Cool!

I think I charged everything

3.

Decision time. You've got a stack of bills in sight with deadlines fast approaching, and you've already maxed out your credit card. But concert tickets for a band you pretty much need to see (if there's going to be any meaning in your life) are going on sale tomorrow, and are likely to sell out pretty fast. What's it gonna be?

worth it? not really...

A. Grab the tickets while you can, put off paying your bills for a week or so, and hope you get a bonus at work, or maybe stumble across a suitcase full of gold ingots in order to cover your late fees.

B. Pay the bills on time, and then start a letter-writing campaign to get the band to come back in a few months for another concert. Maybe you'll be able to catch them next time.

C. The perfect solution! You'll write checks for the bills and put them in the mail, while also ordering up some concert tickets. By the time they cash your checks, you'll definitely have found that suitcase of gold ingots, and it'll be no problem.

4.

IRA is:

A. Your plumber.

B. A type of retirement account.

C. The branch of the government that deals with taxes.

5.

You thought the Mountain Landscape checks from your bank were cool, wait till you see this: Your credit card company is sending you "courtesy checks," which you can use to draw against your line of credit. And not a moment too soon, since you're running low on the old Mountainous Landscape. Next time you're caught in the checkout lane with an empty wallet, you:

A. Dash off one of the credit card checks—you figure they're just like using your credit card, except you get to show off even more of your bold and original handwriting.

B. Stick to your debit card if possible, or just use the credit card and plan to pay off the balance before the end of the month, when interest will start being tacked on. Why bother with those credit card checks since there's always an extra fee?

C. Hand the cashier one of the checks, saying, "Can you fill this out for me? They're running an *A-Team* marathon on cable, and I'm in a hurry to get home."

The right answers are ... B!

(Okay, so maybe Ira *is* the name of your plumber, but come on—did you really think that's what we meant?) Give yourself one point for every B you chose.

4-5 points:

Congratulations—you're on the right track. You know how to avoid the big credit card traps, and you're watching out for the future. But don't stop now—take advantage of the tips in this book to make the most of all your hard-earned cash!

2-3 points:

You're trying, we'll give you that. But unless you've got a really hot lead on that suitcase full of gold, you may have some tough lessons ahead. You'd better get comfy and start reading if you don't want to learn those lessons the hard way.

0-1 points:

So, um, you don't actually have any checks or credit cards in your possession at this point, right? Right??!! Because if you do, you'd better put them down and step away from the checkbook until you've finished reading this book.

ALL ABOUT

ONCE YOU HAND YOUR CASH OVER TO A BANK, YOU PRETTY MUCH HAVE TO PLAY BY THEIR RULES.

CHECKING AND SAVINGS ACCOUNTS

Is your definition of a savings account that wad of cash you stuck in the most original of spots—under your mattress?

Some people get freaked out at the idea of handing over their money to a big scary business they don't know much about, but the wonder of banks is that they can not only make your life easier, they can also make you money.

But once you hand your cash over to a bank, you pretty much have to play by their rules—so it's a good idea to know what the rules are.

Here's a crash course in everything you need to know about checking and savings accounts.

HOW TO CHOOSE A BANK ACCOUNT

Let's start with the basics, just in case you've been living on another planet or ensconced in an alternative structure at the south pole for the past eighteen years. In other words, in case you missed it: The two main types of bank accounts you can open are checking and savings. You'll probably want one of each, since the features vary.

CHECKING

You use this type of account to deposit checks, write checks to pay your bills, and make cash withdrawals. With a checking account, you can get a debit card—but you might want to think carefully about that. More about debit cards on Page 40. Some checking accounts pay interest, but it's usually a teeny tiny amount. That's why you'll want a savings account, too.

SAVINGS

Ten points if you've already figured out that savings accounts are for...duh... longer term saving. You earn a percentage of interest on the money you keep in the account, so the idea is to leave that money alone and stick with deposits, not withdrawals. These accounts are pretty straightforward—you're looking for a decent interest rate and you don't want the bank to make you pay for the "privilege" of leaving your money there. (After all, they're using your money when you're not.) So you want low or no maintenance fees.

40 minute drive to the ATM!

Before you open up a checking account, you'll want to think about three things:

1. **What features do you need in the account?**

2. **How much is it going to cost you to have this account?**

3. **How convenient is the bank, in terms of branch locations, hours, and ATM's?**

Deciding where to bank is a matter of juggling those three factors—features, cost, and convenience—to get the best deal that meets your needs. You probably don't want to choose a bank with great rates and no fees if that bank has no ATM's within a 60-mile radius, for instance. (Otherwise, you'll wind up making just one huge withdrawal each month, and then you're back to stashing your cash under your mattress—which pretty much defeats the whole purpose of using a bank.)

Here's a quick look at the issues you'll want to consider before you choose a bank.

Read on! →

CHECKING ACCOUNT TYPES AND FEATURES

Most checking accounts allow you to write checks, make deposits, and use ATM cards that often function as debit cards as well. Many will also allow you to do online banking.

Sounds simple, right?

But wait till you start trying to sort through the different types of accounts offered by each bank. Each bank has its own set of fancy names for their accounts, but they all boil down to 4 main types:

Basic checking
Discount checking
Premium checking
Online-Only checking

The main differences among them are all about monthly fees and minimum balances. Here's an overview of what to expect, in general, from each type.

BASIC CHECKING

A basic checking account may have no minimum balance requirement, but you pay for just about everything. Some banks will charge you for every check you write; others charge a monthly account maintenance fee of between $10 and $20, and/or they limit the number of checks you can write each month. Some basic accounts will waive the fee if you do maintain a minimum balance—but if you can handle that, you might be ready to move up to a slightly better account that offers more services for free.

not this kind of online!

DISCOUNT CHECKING

This type of account appeals to budget-minded people because it keeps your monthly fees to a minimum. The catch is that you're only allowed a certain number of transactions each month. Each check you write, ATM withdrawal you make, or deposit you make is counted as one transaction. Make sure you can really stay below the allowed number before you sign on for one of these, since the fines for exceeding the limit can add up fast. Note that some budget accounts charge you every time you visit a teller, too.

PREMIUM CHECKING

For the premium checking account, you'll have to maintain a large minimum daily balance—often $5000 or more. In return, you'll get unlimited free banking privileges, including free checks, free online banking and bill paying, unlimited use of tellers, and free use of other banks' ATM's—not just your own. If you let your balance fall below the minimum, though, you'll pay a steep monthly fee—often $20 or more.

ONLINE-ONLY CHECKING

The more banking you do electronically—bypassing the human element and skipping right past all those pesky tellers' salaries—the happier the banks are and the more they save. Many banks now pass their savings along to you by offering an online-only account at a very low monthly fee. Oddly enough, you don't get any checks at all with this type of checking account! But you are able to pay your bills electronically, transfer money from one account to another, and use ATM's. If you go with an online-only account, you'll need to have your paychecks deposited electronically, through direct deposit, rather than by paper checks.

more account types →

student accounts are great!

STUDENT/SENIOR CHECKING

Many banks offer sweet deals to students and seniors—basic no-frills checking accounts that come with benefits like free personal checks, free traveler's checks or cashier's checks, wider ATM use (for reduced or zero fees), better rates on loans and credit cards, and discounts on other items, like travel or prescriptions.

INTEREST-BEARING

If you're blessed with a large chunk of cash and know you'll be able to keep a steady flow of big money coming into your account, then you can open a checking account that also earns interest. You'll have to meet a minimum balance requirement, and maintain an even higher minimum balance on a daily basis to avoid fees. Some of these accounts give a higher percentage of interest on higher balances. But don't kid yourself: the interest rate on these accounts isn't very high, and will never be as high as the interest you could get elsewhere.

CREDIT UNIONS

If you're looking for a real deal, find out if you're eligible to open an account at a credit union. A credit union is a lot like a bank, except that it's a non-profit organization owned and run by its members for the benefit of all. Credit unions are usually available to people who work for the government, are members of labor unions and trade groups, or are employed by very large companies with thousands of employees. The good news is that credit unions offer accounts with the lowest fees and pay a higher rate of interest than many banks. (They also offer lower rate programs for home and auto loans.) The bad news is that you can't join a credit union unless you qualify—usually either through your job, or because you have a relative who already belongs. You might be able to join a local community credit union if there is one in your community.

SPECIAL BANKING SERVICES

Once you've got an account, your bank can provide a number of other services you may need from time to time, including cashiers or certified checks, travelers checks, wire transfers, and stopping payment when you lose a check or in other circumstances. For explanations of when and how to use these services, visit www.realuguides.com.

paying bills on the beach

SMALL VS. LARGE BANKS

You'll also want to consider whether you're interested in the personal service of a small neighborhood bank, or the convenience and financial benefits of a national bank. The tellers and account executives at a local bank will get to know you, which makes it easier if you need them to help you out with tricky stuff like reversing bank charges, eliminating fees, looking up a lost check, or faxing an additional copy of a bank statement. On the other hand, small banks may pay lower interest rates on savings accounts than national banks do. And small banks have fewer ATM's. It's also hard to know for sure whether a small bank is in good financial shape. Going with a big-name bank for its history and success is usually a safe bet.

INTERNET-ONLY BANKS

An alternative to opening an online-only account at a traditional bank is an online-only bank. These Internet banks often have the very lowest fees around, and the upside is that you may get certain services for free that other banks would charge for. You might also earn a higher rate of interest on savings accounts.

But the obvious downside is that the bank won't have any physical branches you can walk into, if problems do arise. And Internet-only banks don't have their own networks of thousands of ATM's nationwide. They'll usually give you an ATM card with a logo that allows you to use it at any ATM machine with the same logo, but you may have to pay a fee each time you use one of these machines to get cash.

CONVENIENCE & MORE

Once you know what kind of accounts work best for you and which banks offer them, check around with friends, relatives, and neighbors to see if they're happy with their banks.

You can also use the web to shop around for the best deals—many major banks have web sites that spell out the details for each type of account. Always look for:

LOCATION, LOCATION, LOCATION

You want a bank that has branches convenient to where you live and work.

FLEXIBLE HOURS

Does the bank open early on certain weekday mornings, stay open late on certain weekday evenings, or provide good weekend hours? Make sure there's at least one day a week when it would be easy to mesh your schedule with the bank's for in-person banking.

"FDIC" OR "NCUA"

You want a bank that is insured by the Federal Deposit Insurance Corporation or the National Credit Union Administration's insurance fund. Why? Because those signs mean that the federal government will protect your deposits, up to $100,000 per account, if the bank goes broke. (Banks can go broke? A scary thought, but true.)

TONS OF ATM'S

The more ATM's a bank has in its network, the better. Otherwise, you'll be stuck paying another bank's fees when you're forced to use an out-of-network ATM. These fees can run from $1 to $3 per visit. If you make 2 ATM withdrawals per week, and you always use an out-of-network ATM, you could wind up paying $24 a month just for ATM use! That adds up to the price of a plane ticket, over the course of a year.

AT A SMALL BANK, YOU MAY GET FRIENDLIER SERVICE.

It's Not a Marriage

One thing you don't have to worry about when you're choosing a bank is a lifelong commitment. There's no real benefit to staying with one bank for the long-term, so your bank doesn't have to be Mr. Right—just Mr. Right Now. If you move, you might find a different bank's branches are more convenient to your home or job, for instance. The most important thing for your future is to make sure you keep your account(s) in good shape with whichever bank you choose.

HOW TO OPEN AN ACCOUNT

Okay, you've done some research (and maybe gone online) to pick a bank and settle on a type of account. Here's what you need to do next:

1. Go into a branch of the bank and bring money—either cash, a paycheck, or a check made out to you from another checking account. (If this is your first checking account, the first deposit might come from your parents.) Find out in advance what the minimum amount is for opening an account. It's usually $100.

2. You'll also need a social security number or taxpayer ID number, driver's license or state ID, and proof of where you live (a copy of a bill mailed to you should do the trick).

3. Sit down with a bank officer and get ready to make some choices. You'll have to decide whether to sign up for overdraft protection, a kind of insurance against bounced checks offered by most banks. With overdraft protection, if you ever write a check and don't have money to cover it (which would only happen totally accidentally, right?), the bank more or less lends you the money until you can make a deposit and catch up. That way the check won't bounce—and you really don't want to bounce a check. If you do bounce one, you get charged fees from both your bank and the other party's bank, plus a load of hassles, and a possible ding on your credit history. If you opt for overdraft protection, you might have to pay a regular fee for it (which means you're out that fee even if you never bounce a check), or you might just have to pay the bank a certain fee when or if a check bounces.

plain checks are cheaper

IT MAKES A LOT OF SENSE TO HAVE YOUR CHECKING AND SAVINGS ACCOUNTS AT THE SAME BANK

4. Choose your checks. When you open an account, the bank will give you a small packet of "starter" checks—just to get you started (unless you're planning to do all your banking online, which is an option). But you'll need to order printed checks with your name and address on them. The bank will make it seem like your only option is to buy the checks directly from them, but you can save some money if you get your checks online or through ads you'll find in the back of the magazine section of your local newspaper. Check out www.realuguides.com for a list of recommended places to buy your checks. (To protect your identity, never put your Social Security number or telephone number on your checks. If a retailer needs your telephone number, you can write it in.)

5. Sign up for online banking. These days most banks allow you to go online for basic account management at least. You can do a lot online, including reconcile your checking statement (which means compare all the transactions listed by the bank with the ones you've written down to make sure you're not missing anything, and that you and the bank agree about how much money you have). You can also transfer cash between accounts if you're

opening more than one at the same bank, and check on electronic direct deposits. If you're an online addict and you'd like to do all your banking online—including paying bills—then find out now if the bank offers that option, and what you need to do to log on.

6. Choose a debit card or ATM card. Virtually every checking account these days comes with an ATM card. Most ATM cards are also debit cards, which you can use to make purchases the same way you'd use a credit card—except the money shoots straight out of your bank account. If you'd rather not have a debit card, make sure you let the bank know to keep your card strictly ATM. See more about debit cards on Page 40.

7. Consider opening another account. It makes a lot of sense to have your checking and savings accounts at the same bank. Some banks with minimum balance requirements will count both accounts toward the minimum, so you don't have to worry about keeping your checking account stocked if you've got enough in the savings. You can also transfer money from one account to the other for free when you need to.

21

4 WAYS TO AVOID BOUNCING CHECKS

Once you've got your account opened, there are a few things to remember on a day-to-day basis.

Boing!

1 Wait for deposits to clear.

The money you deposit on Monday won't actually show up in your account until Tuesday, Wednesday, or later, so don't assume that you can write a check against that deposit until you're sure the bucks are in your account.

■ Find out from the bank what their policy is on "funds availability"— their fancy name for "we've got the money and you can't have it until we say so." Many banks will let you draw a certain portion of the expected money on the same or next business day, holding the rest until the check clears.

■ You'll get the cash faster if it's a federal, state or local government check; a certified check, bank check, or traveler's check; a check from someone who uses the same bank; or an electronic funds transfer.

■ On the other hand, if you just won the lottery, that check for $99 million might not clear for up to 21 days. Banks have a way of being extra careful when it comes to very large deposits.

On the check:
5ik Work Work
421 Labor Ave.
Your Town

pay to the order of

Memo

[BOUNCED]

00678911

Date: _____ 678911

$ _____

Dollars

: 7883403749342: 14 12 77 43 2

The Boss

Balance your checkbook. 2

Balancing your checkbook just means making sure you're always keeping track of everything that goes in and out of your account, even transactions that haven't been processed yet by the bank.

■ The first step is to keep a constant record of every single deposit you make, and every penny that comes back out—whether it's a cash withdrawal, a check paid, or a debit card purchase. Your checkbook has a transaction log where you can write down the date, the type of transaction, and the check number if it's a check you're writing someone. The far right column is for your balance, which you should update by doing the math every time there's a transaction.

■ Remember: Just because the screen on that ATM machine says you've got $153 in there, it might not be true if you just mailed out gas and electric checks the day before. If this happens, the machine will give you money you don't actually have. Then the gas and electric bill payments bounce.
Oops.

> **For great tips on how to use a checkbook register, go to www.realuguides.com.**

Reconcile your bank statement 3

Remember your ATM's 4

When your monthly bank statement comes in, that's when you "reconcile" your checkbook—basically, compare notes and see if everything the bank says you did matches up with what you wrote down. You may have forgotten to write down your monthly account maintenance fee, or a debit purchase you made at the grocery store or gas station, so now you can fill in the blanks. Be sure to read every statement super closely, since there's a time limit (60 days) on how long you have to report a problem. Don't be afraid to speak up if something doesn't seem right, and you're certain you recorded every one of your transactions. It's totally possible that the bank made a mistake somewhere—or you may be a victim of fraud.

Since ATM cash withdrawals are one type of transaction that's especially easy to forget to write down, figure out a system to help you remember. Here are a few ideas:

■ When possible, carry your checkbook register with you and never make an ATM withdrawal until you've written it down.

■ Keep a paperclip attached to your ATM card. When you make an ATM withdrawal or a debit card purchase, clip the receipt to your card. When you get home, enter the amount into your checkbook register. This only works if you remember to look at your ATM card when you get home, though.

■ Put your ATM receipt in your pants pocket, where you keep your house keys. When you get home and take out your keys, you'll feel the receipt. Write down the amount of the withdrawal immediately.

BOING AGAIN

You can get hit both coming and going by bounced checks. If you write a check and it bounces, your bank will charge you a fee unless you have overdraft protection—but even that won't keep you from getting sacked with additional "returned check" fees by the store or company to which you made out that bad check. You'll also get charged by your bank if you try to deposit a check and it bounces. The moral? Make sure your friend has enough cash to cover that fifty he's lending you, or else get ready to pay up.

IT'S EASY TO FORGET
YOUR ATM WITHDRAWALS
AND THEN...BOING!
YOU'VE BOUNCED A CHECK.

ATM
SAFETY TIPS

1. Avoid withdrawing money alone at night in dark areas.

2. Choose ATM's that are inside larger establishments, like grocery stores.

3. Never leave your receipts behind.

4. Shield the keypad with your other hand while you type in your PIN.

6. Look out for someone with an open camera/cell phone who could be videotaping your PIN.

7. Keep an eye out for anyone suspicious, and if you're at all concerned, go somewhere else.

8. Put the ATM card and cash in your purse or wallet immediately. Don't carry it exposed in your hand.

hide your PIN

BANKING AND PAYING BILLS ONLINE

Receiving your bills electronically and paying them online offers a bunch of advantages over writing out checks. When you e-pay:

bank in curlers

- You don't have to worry about snail mail delays.

- With some systems, you can download your bill payment information directly into Quicken or Microsoft Money, two financial software programs that help you track your personal finances.

- You save the cost of postage.

- You may get a financial bonus from your bank.

- You'll cut down your risk of identity theft by reducing the paper trail.

- You can set your account to auto-debit on a specific date, avoiding more late fees (as long as you keep enough $ in your account).

- If auto-debit freaks you out, you can choose to receive e-mail reminders about bill deadlines to make sure you pay on time.

- You can track your payment history online, sometimes for as long as 18 months to 2 years (or longer).

- You'll still get your bank statements in the mail, showing what was paid and when.

If you're not ready to sign up for an e-pay service, you can still pay hundreds of bills online for free simply by going to the company's websites. All major credit cards (Discover, American Express, Visa, MasterCard, Diner's Club) accept electronic payments for free, as do many department stores, gas stations, utility and insurance companies.

Quicken and Other Financial Software Programs

It's happened to all of us at least once: The butler you hired to manage your finances and tidy up around the house resigned in a snit, leaving you to do everything yourself. And although you could simply write the checks and pay the bills by hand, you can't help wondering: Isn't there an easier way?

Well, programs like Quicken, MS Money, and others may be just the answer to those pesky butler problems. They allow you to keep track of your entire financial life—checking and savings accounts, credit cards, mortgages, and investment accounts—with minimal effort and almost no addition or subtraction on your part. The most basic feature of these programs is an electronic version of your checkbook register—you type in your deposits and withdrawals and it totals them up for you. But these programs get really useful when it's time to reconcile your register with your bank statement. You can download bank and credit card statements directly into the program's electronic register—or just enter your closing balance from the paper version of your statement—and bingo! The program will balance your checkbook for you.

Financial software is also useful if you're designing a budget. Once you've downloaded all your transactions or entered them into the register manually, you can divide them into categories like "Transportation," "Food," and "Entertainment." Then the program will draw up pretty charts and graphs to illustrate exactly how and when you've been blowing your hard-earned cash.

Other advantages to financial management software include:

■ Even if your financial life is very simple now—maybe you just have a checking account—mastering a program like Quicken will make it easy to add a 401(k), mortgage, money market, or any other account in the future, when keeping track of your finances on paper is likely to become more difficult.

■ By consolidating all your various accounts in one spot, financial software programs give you an overall picture of your financial situation.

■ Come tax time, you can export all this information directly into tax return software like TurboTax or TaxCut, so doing your taxes is easy.

■ Software makes your financial records ultra-portable. Instead of toting around boxes of old checks and bank statements, all you'll need is a CD.

Like any new technology, there's a bit of a learning curve at the beginning. But once you've mastered the basics, you'll save a lot of time, particularly as your financial life grows more complicated. After all, it's getting harder and harder to find good butlers these days.

Are you one of those pack rats who still has every single math quiz from second grade, or a trigger-happy trasher who accidentally threw out your birth certificate?

Even if you're somewhere in between, chances are you could use a primer on what to toss, what to shred (so no one gets a glimpse of your personal info), and what you really should keep for a long, long time.

FEDERAL AND STATE TAX RETURNS

Keep your tax returns forever. The IRS can do an audit on your return up to 3 years after the filing date, or indefinitely if they suspect fraud (as opposed to an honest error).

MORTGAGE AND HOME EQUITY LOAN MONTHLY STATEMENTS

Shred the monthly statements after you've paid them. Keep the annual statements. You'll need them for your tax return.

PROPERTY TAX STATEMENT

Keep this. You'll need it to complete your tax return.

HOME PURCHASE/SALE RECORDS

Keep these for seven years after you've sold your home.

Don't shred the mortgage!

WHAT TO SHRED?

HOUSEHOLD RECEIPTS

Toss after paying the bills. If you enter receipts into an electronic financial software program, toss after you log your payments. Keep any receipts for major purchases which you may need for insurance verification.

UTILITY BILLS

Shred after payment.

MEDICAL RECORDS

Keep your medical records for one year after the insurance adjustments have cleared and the bills have been paid.
If you have extraordinarily high medical bills and will be claiming a deduction on your federal and state tax return, or if you're being reimbursed for your medical bills by your employer, keep the bills for 7 years after you file the tax returns. Then, shred everything that has personal financial information on it.

INSURANCE POLICIES

Keep all of your insurance policy paperwork for at least three years after cancellation of the policy. After three years, shred all documents that contain your personal information, such as your name, address, phone number and Social Security number. The other documents can be tossed.

INVESTMENT INFORMATION

For tax purposes, it's important to know when you bought or sold an investment so you can calculate your profit or loss. You should keep info on the purchase of an investment until you've sold it, and then you may need to attach the receipts to your tax return. If you receive a year-end statement from your investment company, you may be able to use that as evidence of your profit or loss. Then you can shred all of the other docu-

she keeps everything

there's more! —>

Don't keep every piece of mail you've ever received.

RETIREMENT ACCOUNT STATEMENTS

Keep your active retirement account statements in a file or three-ring binder. You'll want to hold onto these for as long as you own the account. Seven years after you close the account (either by liquidating it or transferring the cash to a self-directed IRA), you can shred the documents.

STUDENT LOAN STATEMENTS

Shred the monthly bills after you've paid them. Consumer advocates recommend keeping the annual statements (which tell you how much principal and interest you've paid during the previous year) forever, in case there is ever a dispute about whether you paid.

ATM RECEIPTS

Shred after you make sure the amount you withdrew or deposited matches the amount shown on your monthly bank statement.

CREDIT CARD RECEIPTS

Keep receipts for business, medical, and other tax deductible expenses, and keep any receipts for warranty or proof of purchase. Also keep receipts for large purchases, if you may need to document an insurance loss. Toss all others, after making sure your receipts match your credit card statement. Shred any receipts that contain your full credit card number.

CREDIT CARD STATEMENTS

Make sure all the information is correct, then shred. If you sign up online with your credit card company, you can access your statements electronically for up to 6 months after the payment is due.

BANK STATEMENTS

If you're audited by the IRS, you may need to prove what money went into and out of your checking and savings accounts. Bank statements and checks that have cleared (or photocopies of checks, if your bank sends you a sheet with miniature versions of your checks paid) should be kept for at least 7 years. Then, shred everything.

EXTRA CHECKS FROM CLOSED BANK ACCOUNTS

If you have extra checks lying around from bank accounts you've previously held, be sure to shred them.

Make sure you shred anything with your personal information—shredding is one of the best ways to foil identity theft. For more information on how to prevent identity theft, check out the *Real U Guide to Identity Theft*.

Make sure you shred anything with your personal information— shredding is one of the best ways to foil identity theft.

CHARGE
CREDIT

ALL ABOUT CREDIT CARDS

There are two ways you can go completely wrong with credit cards. The first way involves that cashmere sweater that's been hanging just out of your reach in the window of Bloomingdales, and that new MP3 player you've been needing, and some shoes, and a couple nights out on the town, and maybe another couple of games for your Playstation, and a short trip to Vegas, and...you get the idea.

It's a big mistake to think that owning a credit card entitles you to a life of self-indulgence, leisure, and excess. But it's also a big mistake—and the second way you can go completely wrong—to avoid credit cards entirely. Why? Because if you never have a credit card, you'll never build a good credit score—in fact, you'll never build any credit score at all! This means that when the day comes for you to apply for a car loan or mortgage, the banks will have no way to judge your reliability. And if they aren't sure they can trust you, they may just turn you down.

Plus it's always a good idea to carry a credit card for use in emergencies. And some large purchases are best made by credit card, because that way you're protected if, for instance, the new sofa isn't delivered, or the vacation cruise you bought is from a company that goes out of business.

So buck up, kid—you may not be able to afford that cashmere sweater yet, but with a little restraint and the tips in this chapter, at least you'll be paying at the pump for gas.

So how do you get a credit card when you've never had one before? There are several possibilities.

1. GET A FULL-TIME JOB

"Wait, how do credit card companies know I have a full-time job?" We're not sure either. Frightening as it may be, they have ways of finding people with steady incomes, so if you're a full-timer you'll probably get your share of offers in the mail.

2. GO TO COLLEGE OR GRAD SCHOOL

Credit card companies love students because of their earning potential, and because their parents are probably still willing to pay their kids' bills. So if you're in college, prepare to be bombarded with credit card offers. Don't waste this golden opportunity to start building credit—you may not get the chance so easily again. Sign up for one credit card with a trusted company. Expect a modest credit limit of somewhere between $500 and $1,000 for a student card.

3. TRY FOR THE EASY ONES

Almost anyone can get a department store or gas station credit card, both of which usually have relatively low credit limits. And although just carrying one of these cards won't impress anyone when later you're trying for a Visa or Mastercard, using a card responsibly will. If you get one of these, never charge more than half the credit limit, make your monthly payments on time, and pay off most if not all purchases in full. Also, check to be sure that the store reports your card activity to the three major credit bureaus. Otherwise, you're not building credit at all—you're just building debt.

tons of credit card offers!

FIRST CARD

4. TRY A SECURED CREDIT CARD

A secured credit card is sort of a cross between a debit card and a credit card, allowing you to open a special account in which you deposit a sum of cash, and are then issued a credit card (usually a Visa or MasterCard) to charge against the account. Usually you can only charge up to the amount you've got stowed in the account—especially at first—but sometimes you can charge two or even three times that amount, once you've demonstrated that you're good for it. There are a few things to keep in mind about these cards, however:

- Some secured cards come with ridiculously high fees that cost you more than you're getting. Avoid cards that ask for "processing" or "application" fees, and look for reasonable annual fees and interest rates (APR's).

- Again, make sure the credit company reports to all three major credit bureaus, so you're getting the credit (literally!) for your effort. Also find out if it will be reported as a secured card, which isn't as helpful as if it's just reported as a credit card.

- Ask about interest—the kind you earn. Since your money has been deposited into an account, it should be earning some level of interest, usually along the lines of what a savings account would earn.

- Do your best to pay off purchases in full and avoid carrying a balance on secured cards. Think of the card as a stepping stone to getting an unsecured credit card, so that you can wave goodbye to the annual fee and say hello to a lower interest rate.

5. ASK YOUR PARENT TO CO-SIGN YOUR CARD

You'll have a much easier time getting approved if someone else with a proven financial history signs on with you. That way the credit company knows they'll have someone who can pay the bill if you don't. But remember that you're asking for a pretty big favor. When you sign up together, you're linking your credit with your co-signer's, so if you do miss a payment, you'll be tanking his or her credit along with your own.

maybe Mom will co-sign?

WHAT TO LOOK FOR IN A CARD

The easiest piece of info to focus on when you're choosing a credit card is the interest rate, which you can usually spot right away in huge print at the top of a credit card offer.

But even a super-low interest rate isn't going to be much comfort if you find you've signed up for a card that takes your first-born child when you're late with a payment. Here's what to look for—and what to look out for—when comparing credit card offers:

NO ANNUAL FEE

You shouldn't have to pay an annual fee unless you're splurging for a gold card or some kind of rewards card. (See Something for Nothing on Page 46 for more on rewards and gold cards.) Some cards will charge an annual fee of $15 to $35 to first-timers. Keep your credit rating clean, and you'll be able to dump the annual fee after the first year.

GENEROUS GRACE PERIOD

You want a card that will give you at least 25 days in which to pay off the balance without being charged fees or interest. Don't even consider cards with no grace periods at all, meaning you'll get charged interest from the date of purchase no matter how fast you pay the bill. Grace periods only apply to purchases, by the way, not cash advances. You'll risk watching your grace period shrink or disappear altogether if you're not careful to make your payments on time and in full every month.

LOW REGULAR (NON-INTRODUCTORY) APR INTEREST RATE

The APR is the interest rate you'll pay if you don't pay off your balance by the due date on your bill. Credit card companies offer a range of interest rates—low rates for good customers with perfect credit, and high rates for riskier customers or first-timers. The rates themselves vary depending on the economy, but the number you end up with within the range depends on you and your credit history. It's tough to get the low end on your first card, but you should shoot for somewhere around 13-15 percent. Watch out for the low "introductory" rate—because "introductory" means that when the 6-, 9-, or 12-month honeymoon is over, the rate will skyrocket, and you'll be at the mercy of the credit card company.

LOW FEES FOR LATE PAYMENTS AND OTHER TRANSACTIONS

Late fees shouldn't be more than $20 per late charge, and other fees shouldn't exceed $35. Some companies offer a reduction in late fees for balances under a certain amount, which is always nice. Watch out for cards that charge you fees for closing your account ("account termination fee") or for transferring your balance to another card.

NO—OR AT LEAST LOW— PENALTY APR'S

You don't want to see your APR jump the second you're late paying a bill, or go over your limit. Although you may have a hard time finding a card that doesn't sock with you with a penalty APR, look for a card that at least limits the penalty APR to no more than 20 percent. You should also make sure your APR will go back down after you've made two consecutive payments on time.

FREE ELECTRONIC BILL PAYING

All of the major credit cards typically offer this service, which allows you to pay your credit card bill electronically, and some will auto-debit your checking account on a particular day so you'll never pay late. (But make sure you have the money in your account on that day, so you don't bounce any checks!)

NO ARBITRATION CLAUSE

Some credit card companies will ask you to agree in advance to settle all disputes in arbitration, rather than in court. Don't do it—arbitration is a costly service that *you'll* have to pay for.

CREDIT CARD

Other terms to know and why they're important.

Minimum Monthly Payment

The key word here is "minimum." You've got to pay the minimum each month to maintain a decent credit rating—but guess what? The minimum is so low, if that's all you ever pay, you're going to be in debt for a very long time. Many cards have a minimum that's only 2% of your total balance. Depending on how much you owe and your interest rate, you could be paying off your credit card debt for 30 years! See the "Prepayment Chart" on Page 58 for more details.

Cash Advances

When you withdraw money from an ATM using your credit card, it's called a cash advance. Cash advances come with high automatic fees, usually somewhere between 2 and 4 percent of the amount you're withdrawing. They're also typically subject to higher interest rates and have no grace periods, so the interest starts mounting up from the moment you walk away from that ATM. Try to avoid cash advances if at all possible.

Variable Interest Rate

An interest rate that varies from billing cycle to billing cycle, depending on a specific interest rate index. Some variable rate cards have a floor, however, so that even when the federal rate goes below this number, the card's rate won't. If you're signing on for a variable rate card, make sure you find out if it's got a floor, and what that floor is.

cash advances—my weakness

DICTIONARY:

Fixed Interest Rate

An interest rate that will remain at a fixed number for a certain period of time. This doesn't mean the fixed interest rate you sign on for will never change, however. Credit companies are legally bound to give you just 15 days notice before changing the interest rate on your card—which they can do at any time for no reason. Both fixed and variable rates can also be changed as a penalty anytime you're late on a payment, for example, or go over your credit limit. Sometimes credit companies will even raise your rates when your payment was late on another bill that was reported to the credit bureaus.

Credit Line/Limit

The total amount of money you can charge on the card, assigned by the credit card company. Don't expect this limit to be enforced automatically on their end, however. Credit companies can choose to either deny a purchase that goes above your limit, or let the purchase go through but sock you with a fine. Usually they go for the latter, since it means more money in their pockets. Keep track of what you're spending—by writing down all purchases, checking the balance online, or using a software program like Quicken—to avoid going over your limit. If you're worried that you'll go over your limit for a necessary purchase, at least try calling the company first to see if you can get them to raise the limit. They'll often do it just because you asked!

Balance Transfers

This is what it's called when you transfer a balance owed from one credit card to another credit card, just because the second card offers a better deal (lower interest rate). Beware that some cards charge a fee for every balance you transfer to the card. Also, make sure you keep paying at least the minimum payments on your old card until the transfer has taken effect, so you don't end up with extra fees that could have been avoided.

Billing Cycle

The time from one bill to the next. Usually, you have until the end of a billing cycle to pay off every credit card purchase made since the start of the cycle without any interest being added on.

Revolving Account

Most credit cards work this way, allowing you to pay only part of your balance each month instead of the full balance.

Charge Account

Charge cards must be paid off in full at the end of each month. The standard American Express card is a charge card.

DEBIT VS.
CREDIT CARDS

Those little pieces of plastic look a lot alike, but there's a world of difference between them, so don't make the mistake of mixing them up. Here's how to keep it straight:

Debit cards are almost like paying with cash...

In other words, the transaction will only go through if you've got the money available in your bank account to cover the purchase, and the funds are taken out of your account right then and there. (Of course, you—and the little computer the clerk is using—might think you've got enough because a check you wrote someone hasn't been deposited or cleared yet, so make sure you're keeping track.)

Credit cards work like mini-loans...

You can use credit cards to buy as much as you want up to a limit set by the credit card company, without having to cough up the cash right away. All you'll need to do is make a minimum payment on the balance every month. The catch? You have a certain amount of time to pay off purchases without any interest (called a grace period), but if you don't meet the deadline, interest gets tacked on to your balance and keeps growing every day. You'll eventually be spending more— sometimes a lot more—than whatever the purchase would have cost if you'd paid in full up front.

So, should you use credit, debit, or both? Each one has its own pros and cons, and it's really about figuring out what's right for your needs.

debit or credit?

DEBIT CARD
YAYS AND NAYS:

The Yays:

■ Debit cards are an easier way to spend "real" money than carrying around tons of cash, which isn't always safe, or writing a lot of checks, which aren't accepted everywhere.

■ When you use a debit card, you won't end up stuck with a scary high bill at the end of the month from all those not-so-little-anymore purchases that you'd totally forgotten about.

■ You also won't be saddled with interest that makes things more expensive than they should have been.

The Nays:

■ Debit cards won't be much help if you don't have the funds in your account to back them up.

■ Some stores refund returned debit card purchases with store credit, when the charge would have just been wiped off a credit card bill.

■ While you're technically protected against fraud, if someone misuses your account you'll still be stuck trying to get money back that's already been spent. With a credit card purchase, you have time to dispute a charge before you ever have to lay out the actual cash.

CREDIT CARD
YAYS AND NAYS:

The Yays:

■ Some credit cards offer certain extended warranties and consumer protections that are almost never offered with debit cards. For example, if you buy an airplane ticket using your Discover Card, you'll get free life insurance in case something happens while you're on that flight.

■ Credit cards also give you the luxury to buy now, pay later when it's something really important that can't wait—like a new transmission for your broken-down car, which you need to drive to work.

■ When you use a credit card the smart way—always making your minimum payments on time and keeping the balance at a manageable level below the limit—you'll give yourself a solid credit history which is a huge help in the future.

The Nays:

■ If you don't handle the card responsibly, you could seriously mess with your credit rating and face trouble the next time you try to get your name on an apartment lease, or apply for any kind of loan.

■ It's also easy to get carried away with credit cards—being able to spend money you don't have is super seductive. And hey, what's the problem with maxing out your cards when those monthly minimum payments are so affordable? Read on!

■ After your shopping spree, you'll figure out exactly what the problem is with maxing out your cards—five years later, you may still be paying off that $300 TV which could end up costing you almost twice as much as it would have, thanks to interest.

10 EASY TIPS FOR CREDIT CARD SUCCESS

To get the most out of your credit card, you've got to use it right. Follow these rules and you should be in good shape.

1. LIMIT YOUR NUMBER OF CREDIT CARDS

It's better to have only a couple of credit lines open and use them regularly than to have many credit cards, even if you rarely use some of them.

2. PAY CLOSE ATTENTION TO CHANGES IN YOUR CONTRACT

When a letter comes in the mail warning you of a new interest rate or other change to your credit card deal, it's up to you to learn and follow the new rules so you don't get burned. If anything seems outrageous or unfair, try calling and asking if they'll consider leaving your plan as is. Consider switching cards if the new policy is really unworkable.

3. STEER CLEAR OF CASH ADVANCES AND CREDIT CARD "CHECKS"

Shred those checks the credit card company mails you with your name already printed neatly on top, and never use your card to withdraw cash unless it's a real emergency. The automatic fees and high interest that come with both of these options just aren't worth it.

4. ASK AND YOU REALLY CAN RECEIVE

Once you've shown yourself to be a responsible credit card holder, you're a prime candidate for better interest rates and a higher credit limit. But don't expect the credit company to offer these out of the goodness of their hearts. Give them a call and ask what they can do for you, especially if you've received some better offers in the mail. They want to hold on to your business, so it's likely you can work something out.

5. READ, READ, READ THE FINE PRINT

Then read it again. You need to know every little detail. For instance, if your credit card has been issued by a bank where you keep another account, does the bank have the right to debit that account directly in order to pay off your credit card bill? If you travel, check to see if there are fees for using your card abroad.

hope i've got the cash

6. KNOW WHEN AND HOW TO CANCEL

If you're thinking of canceling a credit card that you don't use much or aren't happy with, wait until you've paid it off to avoid getting socked with a giant interest rate on your leftover balance. You'll also want to wait if you're going to be applying for a mortgage or car loan in the next couple months. If you do cancel, make sure the transaction will be reported to the credit bureaus as "closed at customer's request." Write down the date and the name of the person you talked to, and look out for a written record in the mail.

7. JUST SAY NO TO CREDIT INSURANCE

Credit insurance will cover your monthly minimum payments in the case of unemployment, disability, or death, but you'll have to pay a monthly premium to get this coverage. Do the math and you'll see that those minimum payments are so tiny, the benefit really isn't worth the cost.

8. REPORT LOST OR STOLEN CARDS ASAP

Legally, the zero-liability protection only comes if you report the loss within 24 hours, although most companies will extend that depending on the situation. First make a phone call, then follow up with a letter detailing what happened and providing all the facts about your conversation with the credit company representative. Beware of bogus "fraud protection" offers you receive for your card, since you're probably already covered and shouldn't need to pay extra.

9. GO ONLINE

A great way to stay on top of your credit card activity and avoid late payments is to set up Internet access for your account. Paying the bill online will cut the risk of a check not making it there on time.

10. KEEP TRACK OF PURCHASES

You don't want to face a heart attack at the end of the billing cycle when you discover that you've been socked with fines and other penalties for going over your limit. Try the paperclip trick—each time you use your credit card, clip the receipt to the paperclip and write down the purchase as soon as you get home.

6 Reasons

to check your credit card statement

It's never pleasant to look at your credit card statement—especially when you know you're going to see the evidence of that massive shopping spree. However, much more unpleasant is opening your credit card statement to find evidence of a massive shopping spree that you didn't participate in. Here's why you should read your statement every month from top to bottom:

THEY CHARGED US TWICE FOR THIS TV!

1 You've got 60 days from the date of the bill to report any errors you spot—and errors do happen.

2 The same time limit applies to reporting any fraudulent charges.

3 If you do see something wrong with your bill, it could be a clue that someone's stolen your ID, and the sooner you can put a stop to that, the better.

4 You're also facing a ticking clock if you want to dispute a charge (see sidebar).

5 Make sure you notice if there's a due time as well as a due date on the bill. This is becoming a common practice, leaving people stuck paying late fees because their payments didn't arrive until after the noon deadline on the right date.

6 Is there a difference between the date when your minimum payment's due, and the date when the balance can be paid off without interest? If the interest kicks in before the minimum payment is due, you could end up paying extra interest even if you get your minimum payment in on time.

NOT MY COFFEE TABLE:

HOW TO DISPUTE A CHARGE

Let's say you whip out your card to buy a coffee table on some online retailer's web site. The table shows up on your credit card bill, but months go by, and it fails to show up at your apartment. Or let's say a nice coffee table shows up on your credit card bill, and the only problem is that you never ordered or received one, and you're perfectly happy with the empty milk crates you've been putting your feet on for the past six months. This is when it's time to dispute a charge.

The Fair Credit Billing Act gives you the right to dispute any billing errors you spot on your credit card bill, like a charge for a purchase you never received or never ordered. You can also dispute a charge if you feel you've been treated unfairly by a merchant—like when a product arrives damaged in the mail. Technically the credit company only has to allow this for a purchase of at least $50 that was made in your home state or within 100 miles of your home address, but they'll usually try to work with you even in situations that don't fit this description. The key here is to get everything in writing. Here's what you do:

1 If the problem involves a merchant, you must first try to resolve the dispute directly with the merchant. If it's a no-go in person or over the phone, send a complaint letter to the merchant and mail another copy to the credit company—both by registered mail with return receipt requested. Keep a copy for yourself.

2 The next stage is disputing the charge through your credit company. You'll need to do this in writing within 60 days of receiving your credit card bill. Include in your letter your credit card number, the closing date of the bill, and of course a description of the disputed purchase and what the problem is—and mail the letter to the company's billing inquiries address. This is usually a different address from the one to which you send your payments. Again, play it safe by using registered mail to document when the notice was sent. You don't have to pay for the disputed charge until the dispute's resolved, but you do still have to make the payment on your other credit charges. Once the credit company resolves the dispute, you'll be free and clear if they find in your favor, or you'll have to pay up (along with finance charges) if they decide the merchant's in the right.

SOMETHING FOR NOTHING: ALL ABOUT REWARD CARDS

Many credit cards offer "freebies" for purchases you make with the card. Here's the lowdown on the most common ones:

Frequent Flyer Miles and Hotel Points

Some cards give you a mile for every dollar you charge. But you can bump up your total by flying on the same airline (don't forget to book online to get more bonus miles) and renting cars from companies that are affiliated with that airline. One airline even has a restaurant program that gives you an additional 10 miles for every dollar you charge eating out. Some hotel chains have their own credit cards with bonus points that give you money back when you stay there.

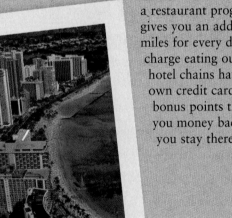

hotel points!

GOING GOLD

You do get some perks with a gold, platinum or titanium card, if you're lucky enough to qualify for one of these. But be aware that it's not always worth it if you're looking at a card that comes with a high annual fee. Here are a few things you might get with a higher-level credit card:

- Lower APR's.

- Higher credit limits.

- Extra insurance for free. Some cards offer up to $1 million in flight insurance every time you buy a plane ticket. You might also get free additional coverage on car rentals, personal liability insurance, protection against lost luggage, cancelled or delayed flights, and sometimes even medical insurance coverage on trips.

- Extended warranty programs. If you buy something on the card and it's lost, stolen, damaged or broken within 60 to 90 days, some gold and platinum cards will replace the item or reimburse you for the cost.

- Travel bonuses. In addition to free trip and travel insurance, some gold and platinum cards offer you free airline tickets, free access to VIP airport lounges, and free assistance in making or changing plans. And some hotel chains will automatically upgrade your hotel room if you check in with a gold or platinum card.

Free or Discounted Gas

Some credit cards give you discounts on gas, like the AAA Visa card, which offers 5 percent off all of your gasoline purchases. If you always buy your gas from the same station, it might pay to get a credit card directly from the chain, like Exxon or Amoco. They usually offer a 3 to 5 percent rebate on your gas charges.

Cash Back

Some cards give you 1 to 2 percent cash back on every purchase. Others limit you to .5 percent or limit the total amount you can charge each year. If you carry a balance, some cards give you as much as 5 percent on the amount of the balance, but at that point you're probably paying 10 percent interest to get 5 percent back. Some cards, like Discover, give you even more cash back if you're using your card to buy something from one of their retail partners.

HOW TO MANAGE

48

CREDIT SO YOU
REALLY
SCORE

Now that you have a credit card, what's next? Hanging onto it, of course, and doing whatever you can to develop a good credit score.

If you think your credit report is kind of like the report cards you got in kindergarten—as in, it's flattering to know someone thinks you "play well with others," but in the long run it's not going to make much of a difference in your daily life—boy, are you in for a surprise.

Fact is, when you apply for a car or auto loan, the first thing the lender wants to know is exactly how well you play with others—namely, those others who have lent you money in the past.

But it goes even deeper than loans. Statistics show that people with great credit are less likely to get into an automobile accident, and they make fewer claims on homeowner's insurance policies, too.

So if you fall into that category, you'll have better luck applying for those kinds of insurance. Landlords typically run credit checks before renting out apartments, and some employers even pull credit reports on prospective employees. Without a credit history, you could be stuck having to pay a hefty deposit for things like your first account with a utilities company.

So don't get sent back to kindergarten. Play well with your credit card companies and they'll play nice with you. (Maybe they'll even invite you to their birthday parties.)

THEY'VE GOT
YOUR NUMBER

Credit scores are numbers that take all these different factors into account and spit out a number that represents your supposed overall financial aptitude and responsibility—sort of like an SAT score for your financial life.

As with the SAT's, you're looking for a high score. Unlike the SAT's, a credit score isn't just one flat number that never changes. Your score can go up and down all the time (although it'll drop down a lot faster than it'll shoot back up). You get points for a history of paying bills on time, and points for keeping your debt-to-income ratio low. Charging up to the max on a credit card will slash your points, and so will bouncing checks.

Many companies offer their own credit score, but the big one—the one lenders and credit card companies use most often—is called the FICO credit score, created by a company called Fair Isaacs.

The FICO credit scores range from 300 to 850. Anything over 675 is considered a good credit score, and anything over 720 falls into the best credit grade. (You'll hear lenders refer to you as having "Grade A" credit or being a "prime" borrower.) If your credit score falls below 675, you're in what's called the "sub-prime" category, and although this is starting to sound like you're a cut of beef, it really means you have less than great credit. If you're a sub-prime borrower, most creditors or mortgage lenders won't offer you the best deal—or any deal at all, depending on how low your number is—because they're less sure about whether you'll repay the loan.

she got a great credit score!

How Your Credit Score Affects Mortgage Interest Rates

Here's an example of how different FICO scores change the interest rate you'd get on a 30-year mortgage, and the extra damage you'd do to your wallet each month from a higher rate.

FICO Score	Interest Rate	Monthly Payment $100,000 loan
720-850	5.685%	$579.45
700-719	5.810%	$587.39
675-699	6.348%	$622.11
620-674	7.498%	$699.08
560-619	8.531%	$771.11
500-559	9.289%	$825.50

WHY YOUR CREDIT SCORE MATTERS

YOUR SCORE: How it Hurts and Helps

AUTO AND HOMEOWNER'S INSURANCE
With a higher credit score, you'll pay lower premiums.

EMPLOYER AND LANDLORD CHECKS
If you have a lot of debt, or a spotty financial track record, you may not get the job or the apartment.

CHECKING ACCOUNTS
Banks are increasingly pulling credit histories before agreeing to open checking or even savings accounts.

HOME LOANS, AUTO LOANS, AND OTHER KINDS OF LOANS
Borrowers with the best credit history and highest credit score pay the lowest interest rates and fees.

CREDIT CARD COMPANIES
Your credit score could get you that zero APR offer, or leave you stuck paying 35 percent.

What Matters Most

■ Your bill paying record, including late payments, bounced checks, and other problems with past bills can have a seriously negative impact on your score.

■ The amount of outstanding debt and number of open credit lines is a negative. High balances on credit accounts and too much credit availability can both hurt you.

■ Having a mixture of credit is considered a positive. You'll nab a higher score once you've got more than one type of credit on your record, including revolving credit like a credit card and installment credit like a car loan.

■ The longer you've been using credit responsibly, the higher your credit score will be.

■ Applying for too much credit at once (except for mortgages and car loans) brings your score down.

the repo man   *your car*

Bad Marks on Your Credit Report

The following things will lower your credit score:

■ You've defaulted on a loan (stopped making payments).

■ You've gone into foreclosure on a home that was mortgaged (the bank takes the house back because you're not making payments).

■ You've had a charge-off (the creditor just gives up on you ever repaying the debt you owe).

■ You've had a car repossessed (taken back by lender).

■ You've gone into bankruptcy.

CREDIT HISTORY: WHAT IS IT?

A credit history is a written record of your financial life. It includes personal information, such as your name, current and past addresses, Social Security number, and sometimes even job info. It also includes a lowdown on all of your credit accounts: which credit cards you have, what your balance is on the cards the day the report was pulled, and whether you pay off your balance on time, or have ever been 30, 60, or 90-days late. It also breaks down the figures on any loans you currently have—mortgages, home equity loans or lines of credit, school loans, car loans, and any personal loans that have been recorded.

HOW TO MAINTAIN GREAT CREDIT

It's all too easy to sink your credit score, but it's a lot harder to bring it back up. Follow these guidelines to keep your score as close to perfect as possible.

1 USE YOUR CREDIT CARD
It's not enough to have a credit card—you also have to use it from time to time. If you don't use your card, some companies will charge you a small fee! Charge $25 or $50 once or twice a month and try to pay it off entirely at the end of the month to avoid interest.

2 PAY YOUR BILLS ON TIME, EVERY TIME
If you can't pay them in full, at least cover the minimum monthly payment by the due date. It only takes one or two late payments to tank your credit score, but you'll need at least a year or two of on-time payments to bring the score back up. (FYI: While it's best to avoid carrying a balance because of the interest factor, your score can be just as high if you're making your monthly minimum payments in full and on time.)

3 DON'T CHARGE TO YOUR MAXIMUM CREDIT LIMIT
Unless you intend to pay off the card completely at the end of the month, don't charge anywhere close to your credit limit. Try to keep your monthly charges or balance to no more than half the limit.

Oops! Maxed out their cards.

4 IF YOU GET TURNED DOWN FOR CREDIT, ALWAYS ASK WHY

The law requires the lender or creditor who turned you down to provide you with a copy of the credit history that sunk your application. Take a close look—it's possible an error found its way into your history, or that your identity has been stolen. You should stay on top of your credit history by checking it at least once a year to make sure everything's correct. If you do spot a problem, begin an inquiry immediately to get the false info off your record.

5 AVOID HAVING TOO MANY CREDIT INQUIRIES AT ONCE

You can request copies of your own credit history without causing any damage to the score. But when a bunch of outside companies pull the history in a short period of time because you're applying for a host of different credit lines, it will show up on the history and could lower your score. One exception: when you're shopping for a mortgage or auto loan, you'll want to shop around, which will mean lots of credit checks in a short time. In this case, multiple credit inquiries won't hurt your score—when you're applying for a mortgage, you can have unlimited credit checks from lenders within 30 days. For car loans, you can have unlimited credit checks within 14 days.

6 KEEP YOUR CARD

In a lender's perfect world, nothing changes. They like to see you living at the same address for years, keeping the same job, and holding the same credit cards. To keep lenders happy, try to keep the same credit cards for years and avoid transferring your balance too often, unless there's an amazing opportunity to get a great interest rate that will last long enough to let you pay off a dramatic portion of your debt. The act of transferring the balance doesn't hurt your score, but frequently opening new accounts and closing old ones can.

How to Get a Copy of Your Credit History and Credit Score

There are three major credit reporting bureaus: Equifax, TransUnion, and Experian. These three bureaus keep the same basic information, but if you get a copy of your credit history from each company, they might look slightly different. Not all creditors report information to every credit reporting bureau, which is why it's smart to get a report from all three. For example, one might show a legal judgment, while another might have a department store's late charge. For more information on how to get your credit report, visit www.realuguides.com.

MANAGING DEBT:

HOW TO PAY IT OFF AS QUICKLY AS POSSIBLE

"Debt" is one of those words that's almost always bad news—kind of like "invasive surgery" or "letter from an ex-girlfriend."

But there are times when debt is necessary, and even useful. For example, when you borrow money to buy something that's going to increase in value, like a house, that's a good reason to go into debt. The same is true when you're financing higher education—the theory being that you'll eventually make more money in the long run if you have a higher degree.

The government seems to agree that these are "good debts," so they give you a tax break by making the interest you pay on home mortgages and school loans tax deductible on your federal tax return. That means you can shave off the interest you pay and deduct it from your yearly income when you file your taxes; the taxes you owe will therefore be lower.

GET RID OF DEBT

Whether it's good debt or bad debt, your goal is always to have the best debt of all—none. Follow these steps to get started:

1 Make a list of all your debts, from those with the highest interest rates to those with the lowest. Make all your minimum payments of course. But take any extra cash you have after that, and apply it toward paying down the highest interest rate, non-deductible debt first. Check out The Beauty of Prepayment below to see how much this can help.

2 Try to lower your interest rates. Keep your eye out for mail offers that would let you transfer the balance on your higher interest rate card to one that offers you nine months or a year at a low interest rate, or maybe even zero interest. Your current credit card company might just match the offer themselves if you call them and threaten to switch.

3 Make your payments on time. The best interest rates go to people with the highest credit score. You'll pay off your debts faster if your interest rate goes down, so do what you can to make that happen.

The Beauty of Prepayment

Minimum payments on credit card bills are typically between 2 and 3 percent of your balance, barely a sliver of what you owe. Meanwhile, the rest of that balance continues to rack up major interest.

By prepaying just a little more on your balance every month, you can slice years off the time it will take you to repay your debt.

Let's say you owe $5,000 on your credit card at 17% interest. If you pay just the minimum payment of $71.28, it'll take you 30 years to clear that debt. And you'll pay more than $20,000 in interest! But look what happens when you pay more than the minimum each month. You immediately start to save a ton in interest payments.

Extra payment each month	Time to pay off debt	Interest paid
Nothing	30 years	$20,702.81
$10/month	12.5 years	$ 6,854.17
$20/month	9 years	$ 4,708.07
$30/month	8 years	$ 3,653.56
$71.28/month (double payments)	5 years	$ 1,961.27

BUDGET TIPS

If you're out of ideas about how to free up the extra cash needed to pay down your debt, try these tips for getting your budget back on track:

■ Sock your bonuses and raises away. Many jobs provide annual bonuses, and almost all offer a raise in your salary every year. Take your bonuses and the extra money from a raise straight to the bank and use it to pay down credit card debt. You might think, "Hey, that's no fun. I just got a raise—I want my standard of living to go up." Well, hey, yourself—it will go up, just as soon as you've paid off all your credit card debt! (No more minimum monthly payments = maxium monthly fun!)

■ Brown bag it. Buying lunch can set you back $5 to $10 a day—more if you skip the cafeteria at work and go to a restaurant. If you make your lunches at home, you can pocket $25 to $50 a week, or as much as $2,600 a year.

■ Turn up/down your thermostat. Making it a little cooler in the winter and a little warmer in the summer can make a big difference on your energy bill. Turning it up or down by 2 degrees can save you at least 10 percent on your bill, or between $10 to $25 per month, and up to $300 annually.

■ Get your hair cut for free. Beauty schools need willing and able volunteers so their students can get some practice. Be a human guinea pig and you could get your hair cut (and in some cases colored) without paying a dime.

■ Make a list before you grocery shop. Write down what you need before you go shopping. That way, you'll spend less time, and less money, in the store. Also, avoid food shopping on an empty stomach. You'll spend as much as 40 percent more if you shop hungry, than if you've just eaten.

■ Make your own gourmet coffee. If you're stopping for a Venti on the way to work, and having another to perk you up mid-day, you're snarfing down at least $10 a day. Instead, buy the beans and make your own java-to-go. You'll save up to $8 a day, or as much as $3,000 a year.

For more great ways to save, log onto www.realuguides.com.

Make your own coffee

59

YOUR MONEY

WHAT TO DO WHEN

See if this scenario sounds familiar—you're lounging on the shore of some beautiful tropical island (you don't own the whole island, but the beach is yours), sipping a delicious fruity concoction, and pondering your biggest problem: How you could ever possibly spend all your billions. No? Us neither. Here's the stuff we wish we'd done during each phase of our lives so we'd be sitting pretty right about now.

spending your billions?

- It's never too early to start saving—especially now, when you're probably not paying rent or other living expenses. Whenever you get some cash, divide it into thirds and immediately put two thirds off the table. One of these thirds should be invested in long-term savings for way down the line. The other third is for bigger expenses coming up in the near future, like college tuition, a special trip or vacation, or maybe a car.

- If you go to college, you'll very likely receive several credit card offers. Take advantage of just one of them in order to start building your credit history. But do your best not to charge more than you can pay off at the end of the month. Your short-term goal is to get out of college with little or no credit card debt and as few school loans as possible.

- If you do have any credit card debt from college or other expenses, pay it off as quickly as possible with every spare cent you have. Once that debt is gone, start paying more than the minimum on any student loans you may have taken out. Sure, they've got lower interest rates than credit cards, but it's still interest!

- Start socking money away for a down-payment on your first home (condo, townhouse, single-family fixer-upper, whatever you can afford in your area). Owning instead of renting means you're getting an investment along with a roof over your head.

- Open up your first retirement account. This might be a Roth IRA or your employer's 401(k) if your employer offers one. Contribute as much as you can to these retirement savings plans. By the time you retire, money invested now will have grown in massive proportions. For more about retirement accounts, see the *Real U Guide to Saving and Investing*.

  - Pay all of your bills on time to keep your credit rating up, which will make you eligible for the cheapest credit card deals and loan programs.

gotta pay for college...

this is the good life!

In your
30's & 40's:

- If you have kids, start saving for their college tuition as soon as they're born. Investigate tax-free investment options the government offers for money that will be used specifically for college tuition.

- Pay down car loans and mortgages as much as possible, to cut down on the amount of interest you'll owe.

- Become an expert at planning inexpensive vacations.

In your
50's, 60's
and beyond:

- The kids are out of college, the mortgage is paid off, and all the saving you've done has left you in great shape. Now you've got options: Retire early, start a home-based business, volunteer, play with your grandchildren, travel, or do something else you love.

MORE REAL U...
CHECK OUT THESE OTHER REAL U GUIDES!

YOUR FIRST APARTMENT

Whether you're leaving home for the first time, heading off to college...or skipping the college thing and sliding straight into a real job and real life, this guide has everything you need to know to move out of the house and start your life for real.

LIVING ON YOUR OWN

So you've finally moved into your first apartment. Now what? Plunge into real life with a safety net. If you can't cook, always shrink your socks, and have no idea where to find your stove's pilot light, this is the guide for you.

BUYING YOUR FIRST CAR

Don't get burned on the first big purchase you make. Find out how to get the best financing, how to avoid the latest scam tactics, whether to buy extended warranties, and more.

FOR MORE INFORMATION ON THESE AND OTHER REAL U GUIDES, VISIT WWW.REALUGUIDES.COM.